SEEDS: Tomorrow Starts Today
Copyright 2020 by Jeff Little

All Rights Reserved. No part of *SEEDS: Tomorrow Starts Today* may be reproduced, stored in a retrieval system, or transmitted, in any form or in any means—by electronic, mechanical, photocopying, recording or otherwise—without permission.
Thank you for buying an authorized edition of this book and for complying with copyright laws.

Unless otherwise noted, all Scripture references taken from The Holy Bible, New International Version®, NIV®. Copyright ©1973, 1978, 1984, 2011 by Biblica, Inc.™ All rights reserved worldwide. www.zondervan.com The "NIV" and "New International Version" are trademarks registered in the United States Patent and Trademark office by Biblica, Inc.™

Scripture quotations marked (ESV) are from The Holy Bible, English Standard Version® (ESV®), copyright © 2001 by Crossway, a publishing ministry of Good News Publishers. Used by permission. All rights reserved.

www.milestonechurch.com
ISBN: 978-0-578-82830-5

Printed in the United States.

SEEDS

Tomorrow Starts Today

POTENTIAL
INTRO PART ONE

PROCESS
INTRO PART TWO

RESISTANCE
WEEK ONE

FAITH
WEEK TWO

MOMENTUM
WEEK THREE

TRANSFORMATION
WEEK FOUR

MULTIPLICATION
WEEK FIVE

LEGACY
WEEK SIX

HERE'S THE PLAN

1.
Grow closer to God as you understand and study His Word.

2.
Study the intro weeks individually. Study weeks 1-6 with a group.

3.
Ensure better tomorrows by making great choices today.

HOW THIS GUIDE WORKS

READ THE CHAPTER
- CONCEPT
- CONTEXT
- WHAT DOES THIS MEAN FOR US TODAY?
- WHAT DO I DO WITH THIS?

INTERACT WITH THE CONCEPTS
- TAKE NOTES IN THE MARGINS.
- WRITE OUT ANSWERS TO THE QUESTIONS.
- MEMORIZE THE WEEKLY VERSE.
  (CARDS LOCATED IN THE BACK OF THIS GUIDE)

TALK ABOUT IT WITH YOUR GROUP

STARTING WEEK 1 – RESISTANCE

INTRO ONE

INTRO PART ONE

POTENTIAL

INTRO PT.ONE

"AS LONG AS THE EARTH ENDURES, SEEDTIME AND HARVEST, COLD AND HEAT, SUMMER AND WINTER, DAY AND NIGHT WILL NEVER CEASE." GENESIS 8:22

SEEDS: TOMORROW STARTS TODAY

CONCEPT

We all encounter moments in life that are filled with potential:

- Counting down the last few moments of one year while looking ahead to the next
- Discovering your letter of acceptance from your dream college
- Landing the job you've been wanting at a company you admire
- Waking up on your wedding day
- Stepping on campus for your first day of school
- Finding out your offer has been accepted on your new house, with visions of renovations and the hopes of lasting family memories

Potential is exciting. It's alluring. But potential can also be fleeting and unfulfilled.

One of the best metaphors for potential is a seed.

Seeds are small, but inside them they carry incredible potential for exponential growth. Inspired by this idea, Ralph Waldo Emerson once wrote, "The creation of a thousand forests is in one acorn."

SEEDS: TOMORROW STARTS TODAY

INTRO PT. ONE

CONTEXT

There are seeds all throughout the Bible. God is a master builder and one of His primary building blocks is the seed. Seeds must be cared for, seeds take time to sprout and grow, and seeds follow a carefully designed system.

This is how God set up the world. From the time dry land emerged at His command, He created all the plants, vegetation, and trees to fill the earth and to bear seeds (Genesis 1:11-13).

He told Adam that every seed-bearing plant on the face of the whole earth and every tree with fruit was given to him for food (Genesis 1:29).

God could have provided food for His people any way He wanted, but He chose this process to help them understand how life works and to develop and build their character.

Later, in Genesis chapter 8, Noah and his family celebrate God's faithfulness and His goodness for saving them through the flood. They're so grateful to be back on the dry ground after being stuck in a boat for so long. In this moment, God reminds them of this process (Genesis 8:22).

GENESIS 1:11-13

11 THEN GOD SAID, "LET THE LAND PRODUCE VEGETATION: SEED-BEARING PLANTS AND TREES ON THE LAND THAT BEAR FRUIT WITH SEED IN IT, ACCORDING TO THEIR VARIOUS KINDS." AND IT WAS SO. 12 THE LAND PRODUCED VEGETATION: PLANTS BEARING SEED ACCORDING TO THEIR KINDS AND TREES BEARING FRUIT WITH SEED IN IT ACCORDING TO THEIR KINDS. AND GOD SAW THAT IT WAS GOOD. 13 AND THERE WAS EVENING, AND THERE WAS MORNING— THE THIRD DAY.

GENESIS 1:29

29 THEN GOD SAID, "I GIVE YOU EVERY SEED-BEARING PLANT ON THE FACE OF THE WHOLE EARTH AND EVERY TREE THAT HAS FRUIT WITH SEED IN IT. THEY WILL BE YOURS FOR FOOD."

SEEDS: TOMORROW STARTS TODAY

INTRO PT. ONE

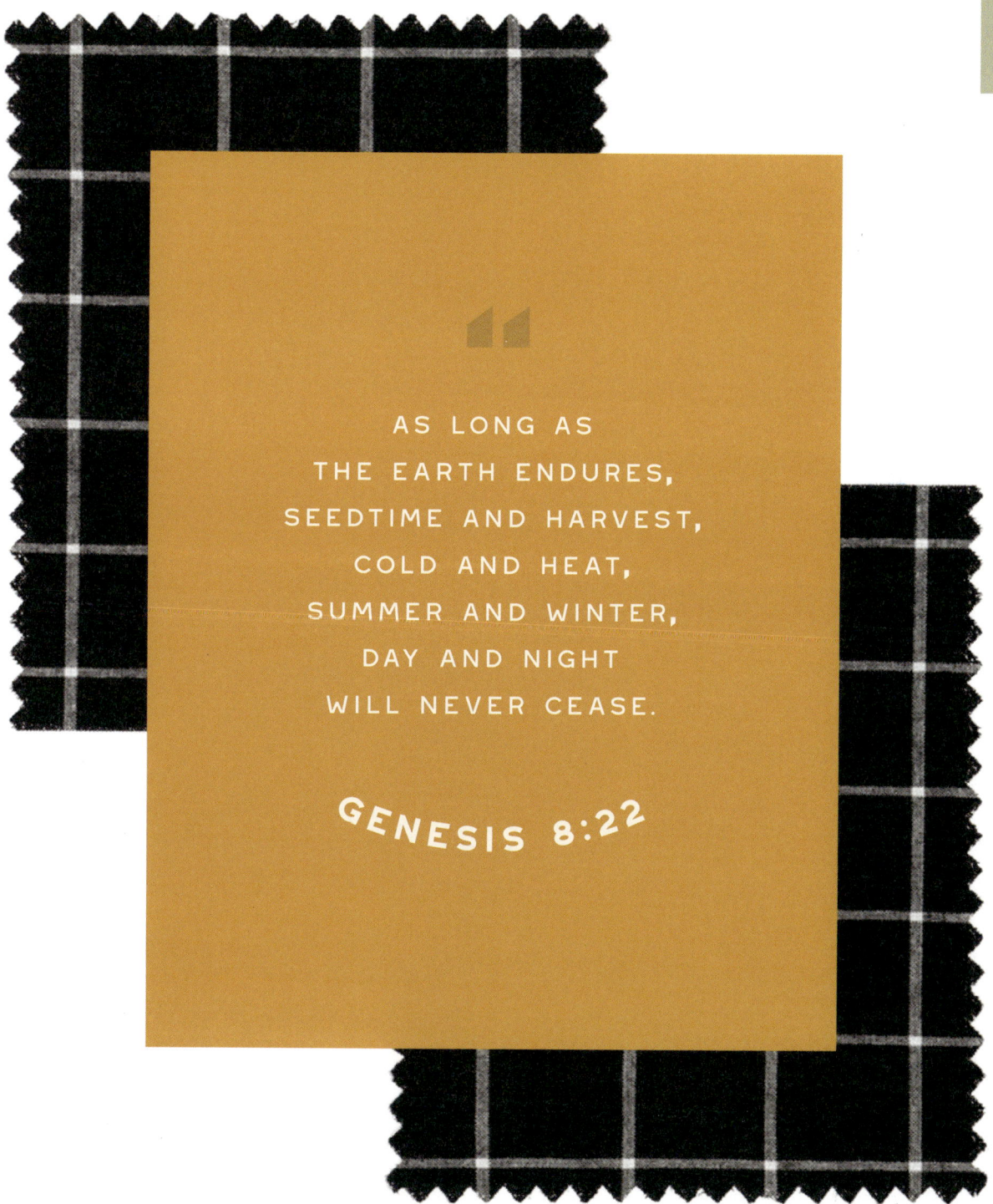

"

AS LONG AS
THE EARTH ENDURES,
SEEDTIME AND HARVEST,
COLD AND HEAT,
SUMMER AND WINTER,
DAY AND NIGHT
WILL NEVER CEASE.

GENESIS 8:22

SEEDS: TOMORROW STARTS TODAY

INTRO
PT. ONE

SEEDS: TOMORROW STARTS TODAY

WHAT DOES THIS MEAN FOR US TODAY?

INTRO PT. ONE

The process of seedtime and harvest may have seemed obvious in the ancient world, but we need to be reminded. Most of us don't live in agrarian cultures; we don't have to understand how the seed works. We can go to the grocery store or order online and have our food delivered.

But no matter where or when we live, and no matter how technology advances, the simple system of seedtime and harvest remains. God wants us to understand and benefit from this process.

Life is seasonal—there's cold *and* heat, summer *and* winter, day *and* night. There's a rhythm to life. Life is not the same thing over and over, and it's not instant.

Potential isn't realized overnight. It takes time and careful attention. It doesn't just happen. This is the power and principle of the seed.

- What you hope for tomorrow begins with the seeds you plant today.

- What you want to see in your relationship with God in a year is formed by the choices you make today.

- What you desire for your marriage is determined by the words, the actions, and the practices you plant today.

- The marriage you hope to have one day begins with the choices you make as a single person today.

INTRO PT. ONE

Seeds are a big deal to God.

We know this because two of the things that are most important to Him—His Word and His Son—are both described as a seed in the Bible.

Have you ever thought about that before? **God describes His Word and His Son as a seed.**

In Isaiah 55, God compares the way His Word comes down to earth with the way rain and snow come down and make every living thing flourish, producing seed for the sower and bread for the eater.

And in John 12, Jesus predicts His own death using the metaphor of a kernel of wheat as a seed. He said a seed that falls to the ground is lost but a seed that is planted becomes many seeds.

God's Word and God's Son both function as seeds. When they're planted, they always bear fruit. It takes time. It's a process, but you can count on them. They always accomplish what they're sent forth to do.

Because of this, any healthy understanding of potential—of how seeds work—always begins with God's Word and God's Son.

Throughout this study, we're going to grow in our understanding of the importance of the seed, how it works, how we make choices today that shape our tomorrow, and how we understand and love God more through the process.

ISAIAH 55:10-11

[10] "AS THE RAIN AND THE SNOW COME DOWN FROM HEAVEN, AND DO NOT RETURN TO IT WITHOUT WATERING THE EARTH AND MAKING IT BUD AND FLOURISH, SO THAT IT YIELDS SEED FOR THE SOWER AND BREAD FOR THE EATER. [11] SO IS MY WORD THAT GOES OUT FROM MY MOUTH: IT WILL NOT RETURN TO ME EMPTY, BUT WILL ACCOMPLISH WHAT I DESIRE AND ACHIEVE THE PURPOSE FOR WHICH I SENT IT."

JOHN 12:23-24

[23] JESUS REPLIED, "THE HOUR HAS COME FOR THE SON OF MAN TO BE GLORIFIED. [24] VERY TRULY I TELL YOU, UNLESS A KERNEL OF WHEAT FALLS TO THE GROUND AND DIES, IT REMAINS ONLY A SINGLE SEED. BUT IF IT DIES, IT PRODUCES MANY SEEDS."

SEEDS: TOMORROW STARTS TODAY

WHAT DO I DO WITH THIS?

INTRO PT.ONE

Think about where you want to be at this time next year:

- IN YOUR RELATIONSHIP WITH GOD - IN YOUR MARRIAGE -
- IN YOUR RELATIONSHIP WITH YOUR KIDS - IN YOUR CAREER -
- IN YOUR FRIENDSHIPS -

Come up with a simple, clear picture. Now, how are you going to get there? That's what we're going to work on through this study together.

You can't make it happen in a day, a week, or even a month, but you can take the first step. And the truth is, you can't take the first step until you know where you're trying to go.

Use the space below to:

1. Write out the most important areas of your life.

2. List practical goals you would like to accomplish in those areas this year.
(Examples: your relationship with God, your marriage, your kids, your friendships, your career, your finances, etc.)

INTRO PT. TWO

"STILL OTHER SEED FELL ON GOOD SOIL, WHERE IT PRODUCED A CROP—A HUNDRED, SIXTY OR THIRTY TIMES WHAT WAS SOWN."
MATTHEW 13:8

CONCEPT

According to Webster's Dictionary, a process is a natural phenomenon marked by gradual changes that lead toward a particular result.

PROCESS 1: A seed gets planted in the ground; it receives water and sunlight; it begins to sprout; it grows to maturity; it's picked; it produces seeds; and the process begins again.

PROCESS 2: A thought becomes an idea; an idea becomes a belief; a belief becomes an action; and the action produces a result.

A process requires time and healthy function. It can break down anywhere along the way.

When we look at the process of a seed in comparison to how our thoughts become our beliefs and eventually our actions, we understand how we grow and change more clearly.

This compare and contrast approach is a common tool in teaching.

Jesus loved this method. Perhaps His most well-known teaching device was the parable. The word "parable" comes from two root words that essentially mean, "to throw alongside." In other words, if someone wanted to illustrate a point, they could include a parable alongside the main point. Parables, then, are short stories, often featuring an unexpected twist, used to illustrate a righteous truth.

One of the most interesting features of parables is the fact that the meaning isn't always obvious. Sometimes they create more questions than answers. The disciples would frequently approach Jesus immediately after He gave a parable to ask for help. Jesus did this on purpose.

Throughout this study, we'll look at the parables of Jesus that relate to the concept or principle of the seed. The first one we're going to look at is one of His most well-known parables. There are nearly identical versions in Matthew, Mark, and Luke. It's known as, "The Parable of the Sower."

SEEDS: TOMORROW STARTS TODAY

INTRO
PT.TWO

CONTEXT

Jesus has been teaching and healing throughout the region. He's chosen His disciples and sent them out to do ministry themselves.

Everyone is trying to understand what He's up to and what His plans are. He had to remind His cousin John the Baptist what His mission was. The Pharisees were accusing Him and challenging His methods.

Even His mom and His siblings were trying to understand why He wasn't around more.

While everyone had opinions and expectations, Jesus continued to clarify His purpose, His Kingdom, and what it meant to have a genuine relationship with His Father.

SEEDS: TOMORROW STARTS TODAY

INTRO PT. TWO

MATTHEW 13:1-9

[1] That same day Jesus went out of the house and sat by the lake. [2] Such large crowds gathered around him that he got into a boat and sat in it, while all the people stood on the shore. [3] Then he told them many things in parables, saying: "A farmer went out to sow his seed. [4] As he was scattering the seed, some fell along the path, and the birds came and ate it up. [5] Some fell on rocky places, where it did not have much soil. It sprang up quickly, because the soil was shallow. [6] But when the sun came up, the plants were scorched, and they withered because they had no root. [7] Other seed fell among thorns, which grew up and choked the plants. [8] Still other seed fell on good soil, where it produced a crop—a hundred, sixty or thirty times what was sown. [9] Whoever has ears, let them hear."

WHAT DOES THIS MEAN FOR US TODAY?

Jesus describes the process of "broadcast sowing" where a farmer took a bag of seed and scattered it across the field. Sometimes they would go back and plow the ground so the seed could go down in the ground. But many times, the farmer simply trusted the process and allowed the good seed to identify itself through its ability to bear fruit.

Jesus ends the teaching with the phrase, "Whoever has ears, let them hear." He doesn't give any detailed explanation. He doesn't tell us what He means by birds or rocky places. In this way, He's following the example of the farmer. He throws out the seed and trusts the process.

And yet, He knew this was a big crowd—this wasn't "Farmers Only." So many people had come to hear Him teach that He had to improvise and go out on a boat in order for everyone to hear.

He's talking about more than growing food. He's talking about how life works.

While it may appear mysterious and confusing to us, "Whoever has ears, let them hear," was a common contemporary idiom Jesus used to separate the casual observer from the engaged follower. Everyone had ears, but not everyone could hear what He was saying. Not everyone was committed to grow.

Jesus is making a big point. Every seed is filled with incredible potential, but in order to deliver, it has to survive the lengthy process.

The same is true for us.

The intention to grow closer to God is powerful, but it doesn't happen overnight.

It grows according to a long-term commitment to an ongoing process.

- *You can't build a healthy marriage with one weekend getaway.*
- *You can't develop trust between a parent and a child by purchasing the most expensive gift they ask for.*
- *You can't build spiritual family by sitting in a worship center a couple of times a month.*
- *You can't equip a young team member with occasional, general feedback.*

You can't separate good seed from bad with a look—it takes a process. In the same way, you separate good thoughts, ideas, attitudes, and behaviors in a process.

Notice in the parable that some of the seed falls on "good soil," and of the seed that falls on good soil, some of that seed produces 100, some 60, and some 30 times what was sown. 30 is good, 60 is better, but we all love 100. Without a process, you don't know how to tell one seed from the other.

Jesus is giving us one of the most foundational and important teachings on seeds in the whole Bible.

INTRO PT.TWO

SEEDS: TOMORROW STARTS TODAY

SEEDS: TOMORROW STARTS TODAY

WHAT DO I DO WITH THIS?

INTRO PT. TWO

Do you have processes in your life to help you reach the potential you came up with last week?

How do you separate good ideas, thoughts, attitudes, and behaviors from bad ones? How do you separate the good ones (30), and the great ones (60), from the best ones (100)?

Two of the most proven processes for decision-making are 1) God's Word and 2) trusted relationships.

This is why this guide is designed for you to study and practically apply God's Word in the context of a Small Group.

COMMIT TO A GROUP OF PEOPLE TO STUDY AND APPLY THESE CONCEPTS WITH FROM GOD'S WORD FOR THE NEXT SIX CHAPTERS.

SEEDS: TOMORROW STARTS TODAY

INTRO PT. TWO

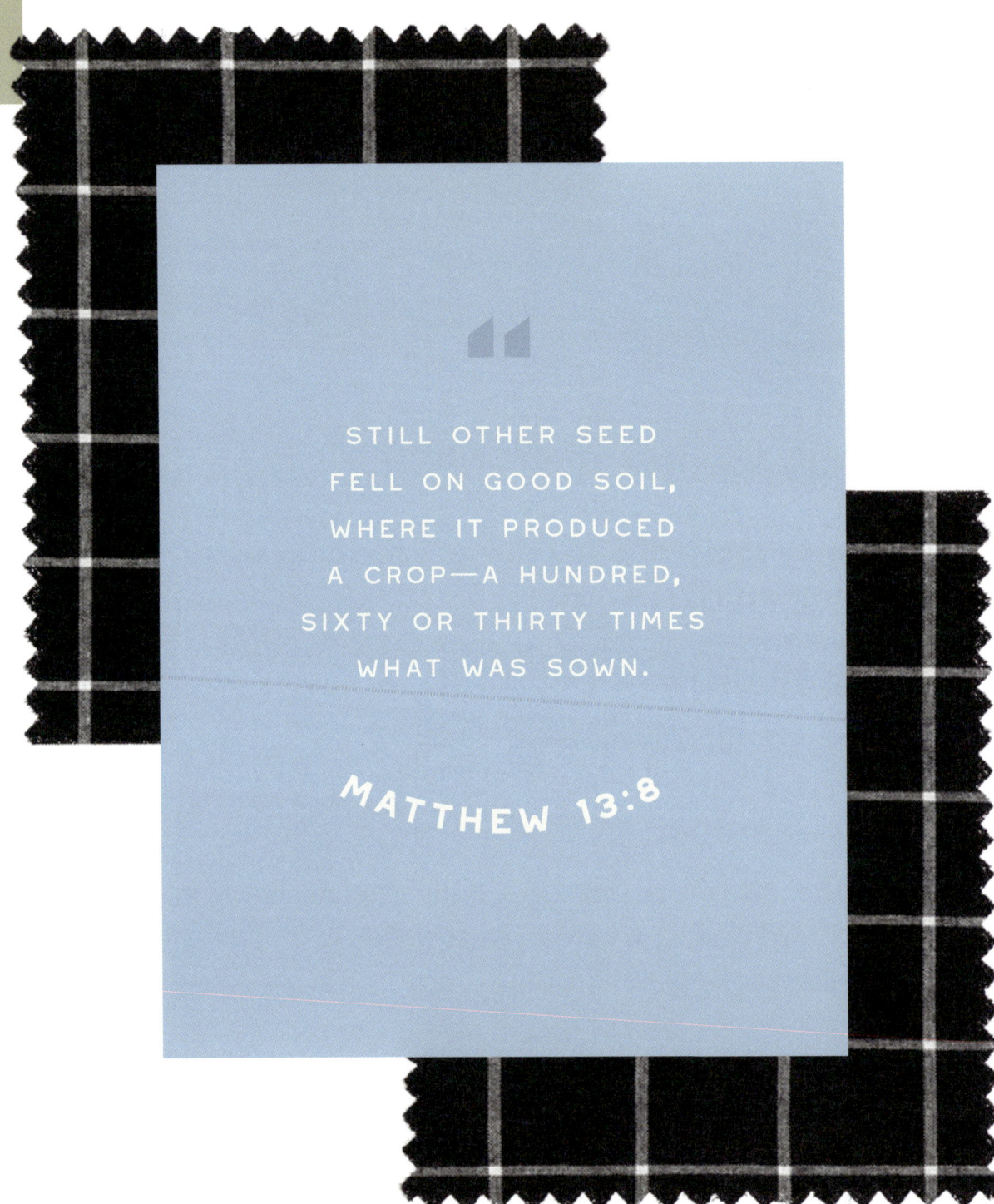

"
STILL OTHER SEED
FELL ON GOOD SOIL,
WHERE IT PRODUCED
A CROP—A HUNDRED,
SIXTY OR THIRTY TIMES
WHAT WAS SOWN.

MATTHEW 13:8

SEEDS: TOMORROW STARTS TODAY

INTRO PT.TWO

SEEDS: TOMORROW STARTS TODAY

WEEK ONE

LET US NOT BECOME WEARY IN DOING GOOD, FOR AT THE PROPER TIME WE WILL REAP A HARVEST IF WE DO NOT GIVE UP.
GALATIANS 6:9

CONCEPT

We like the idea of potential; it's filled with hopeful promise. We even like the idea of process—it gives us confidence in future outcomes. But no one really likes resistance.

We don't choose to be uncomfortable if we can avoid it. We like fast and easy. We want life hacks. We used to wait weeks for a package—now almost everything can be delivered in a matter of hours.

As we grow in our understanding of how seeds work, it becomes clear there are more obstacles than time. There are very real enemies we encounter. Potential often goes unrealized. Processes can break down.

This explains why we can all relate to the frustration of unmet expectations. When we experience the gap between best intentions and actual outcomes, we become discouraged:

- A friend we repeatedly invite to church promises to come but never follows through
- A relationship that seemed so promising ends abruptly
- A passionate desire to grow closer to God slowly drifts into complacency
- A child experiences disappointment and struggle
- An opportunity for promotion turns into the loss of a job
- A career choice produces financial stability but leaves you feeling passionless and unfulfilled

SEEDS
Tomorrow
Starts Today

SEEDS
Tomorrow
Starts Today

SEEDS
Tomorrow
Starts Today

SEEDS
Tomorrow
Starts Today

SEEDS
Tomorrow
Starts Today

SEEDS
Tomorrow
Starts Today

SEEDS
Tomorrow
Starts Today

SEEDS
Tomorrow
Starts Today

SEEDS | Intro Part One

"AS LONG AS
THE EARTH ENDURES,
SEEDTIME AND HARVEST,
COLD AND HEAT,
SUMMER AND WINTER,
DAY AND NIGHT
WILL NEVER CEASE."

GENESIS 8:22

SEEDS | Intro Part Two

"STILL OTHER SEED
FELL ON GOOD SOIL,
WHERE IT PRODUCED
A CROP—A HUNDRED,
SIXTY OR THIRTY TIMES
WHAT WAS SOWN."

MATTHEW 13:8

SEEDS | Week One

LET US NOT BECOME
WEARY IN DOING GOOD,
FOR AT THE PROPER TIME
WE WILL REAP A HARVEST
IF WE DO NOT GIVE UP.

GALATIANS 6:9

SEEDS | Week Two

"TRULY I TELL YOU, IF YOU
HAVE FAITH AS SMALL AS A
MUSTARD SEED, YOU CAN SAY
TO THIS MOUNTAIN, 'MOVE
FROM HERE TO THERE,' AND
IT WILL MOVE. NOTHING WILL
BE IMPOSSIBLE FOR YOU."

MATTHEW 17:20b

SEEDS | Week Three

I PLANTED THE SEED, APOLLOS
WATERED IT, BUT GOD HAS BEEN
MAKING IT GROW. SO NEITHER
THE ONE WHO PLANTS NOR THE
ONE WHO WATERS IS ANYTHING,
BUT ONLY GOD, WHO MAKES
THINGS GROW.

1 CORINTHIANS 3:6-7

SEEDS | Week Four

FOR YOU HAVE BEEN BORN
AGAIN, NOT OF PERISHABLE
SEED, BUT OF IMPERISHABLE,
THROUGH THE LIVING AND
ENDURING WORD OF GOD.

1 PETER 1:23

SEEDS | Week Five

HE WHO SUPPLIES SEED
TO THE SOWER AND BREAD
FOR FOOD WILL SUPPLY
AND MULTIPLY YOUR
SEED FOR SOWING AND
INCREASE THE HARVEST
OF YOUR RIGHTEOUSNESS.

2 CORINTHIANS 9:10

SEEDS | Week Six

THOSE WHO GO OUT
WEEPING, CARRYING SEED
TO SOW, WILL RETURN WITH
SONGS OF JOY, CARRYING
SHEAVES WITH THEM.

PSALM 126:6

SCRIPTURE CARDS

These Scripture memory cards correspond to the memory verse for each week in the *Seeds* study.

We encourage you to memorize these verses during each week of *Seeds*. To help, punch out these cards and put them somewhere visible, like the dash of your car, the back of your phone, or your bathroom mirror.

RESOURCES

MILESTONERESOURCES.COM

FOR MORE RESOURCES VISIT US ONLINE

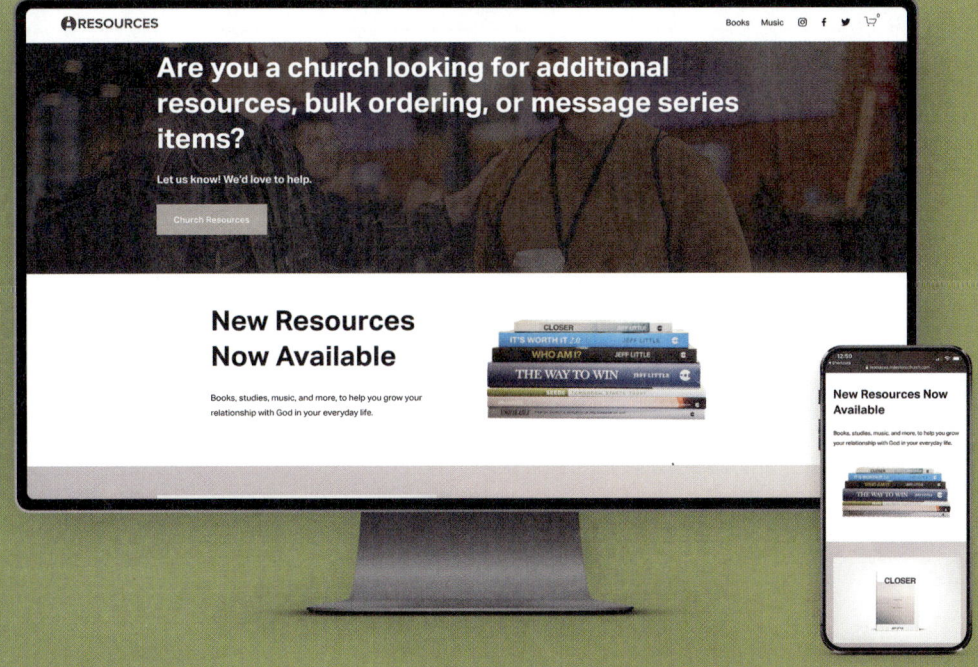

MILESTONERESOURCES.COM

NOTES

SEEDS: TOMORROW STARTS TODAY

NOTES

4 Read John 4:35. What do you think Jesus means when He says that the fields are "ripe for harvest"?

5 Why do you think Jesus tells His disciples to open their eyes and look at the fields? What does that mean for us today?

6 How much do you prioritize God's Kingdom in your life? How much of your life are you sowing into His Kingdom?

7 Let's get practical. Take a few minutes to think about your future legacy. What do you want it to be? And what seeds do you need to start planting today to make that legacy become a reality?

1. How would you define the word "legacy"?

2. Why is it important to think about your future legacy?

3. Do you think there's a difference between a worldly legacy and a godly one? Explain.

SEEDS: TOMORROW STARTS TODAY

WEEK SIX

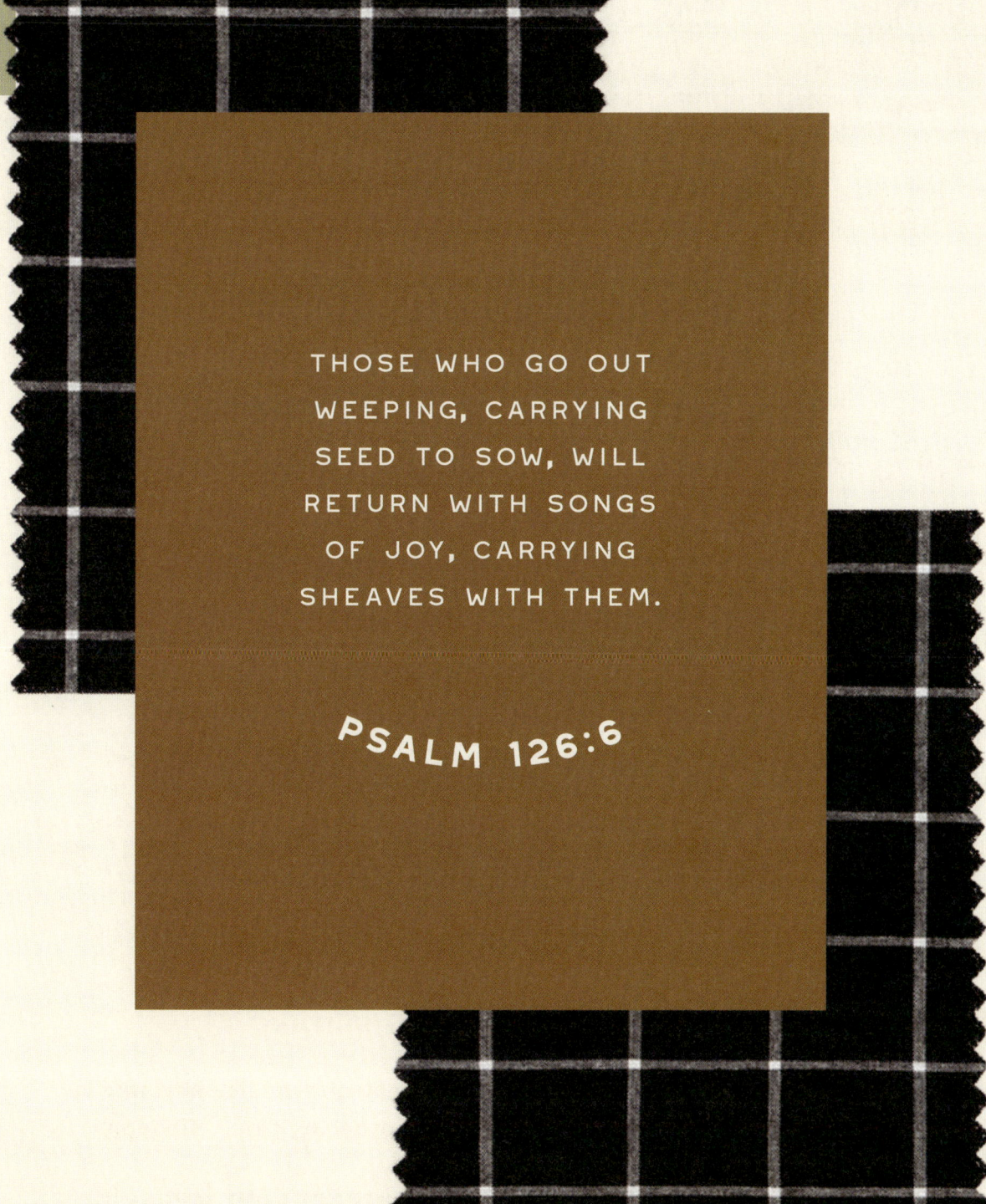

THOSE WHO GO OUT WEEPING, CARRYING SEED TO SOW, WILL RETURN WITH SONGS OF JOY, CARRYING SHEAVES WITH THEM.

PSALM 126:6

SEEDS: TOMORROW STARTS TODAY

WHAT DO I DO WITH THIS?

WEEK SIX

**Every day is an opportunity
to invest in your legacy.**

The words, the time, the consideration,
and the loving service you invest in other people are seeds.

It's easy to take this for granted.
Robert Louis Stevenson said, *"Don't judge each day
by the harvest you reap, but by the seeds you plant."*

- When you read the Bible, you invest in your character.
- When you pray for your children, you invest in their future.
- When you honor God by generously giving your hard-earned financial resources through tithes and offerings, you're investing in your future by trusting God as your source.
- When you choose to limit your schedules so you can go to church together as a family, it may be difficult, but it's an investment in your future relationships.
- When you invite your friend, your co-worker, or your neighbor into a Small Group, you're sowing seed into their eternal future.

It may not seem like anything special. You may not feel like anything is
happening. But you're doing your part in advancing God's Kingdom.

What are you doing today to prepare for your legacy?

Jesus says that in His Kingdom there's a principle that allows us to reap where we haven't sown and to receive the benefit for things we haven't worked for. What an incredible promise: Others have done the hard work, but you receive the benefits of the labor.

This is possible when sowers and reapers join together in the same vision—the harvest. Whenever Jesus talks about the harvest, He's referring to people who are far from God coming into a genuine relationship with Him.

Bible scholars believe Jesus is referencing Amos 9:13 here—a prophetic passage promising a great harvest of God's people.

When we focus on the harvest, when we're less concerned about our reputation and what we get out of it and surrender our desires and significance for the mission of God's Kingdom, we build a legacy.

Jesus said when we seek His Kingdom first, not only will we see it, but we'll also receive everything else God has for us.

Does this mean every one of us is supposed to quit our jobs and work at the church? No. But it does mean we offer our gifts and our resources to help bring as many people as possible into a genuine relationship with Jesus.

AMOS 9:13

"THE DAYS ARE COMING," DECLARES THE LORD, "WHEN THE REAPER WILL BE OVERTAKEN BY THE PLOWMAN AND THE PLANTER BY THE ONE TREADING GRAPES. NEW WINE WILL DRIP FROM THE MOUNTAINS AND FLOW FROM ALL THE HILLS."

WHAT DOES THIS MEAN FOR US TODAY?

Once again Jesus is using the metaphor of seeds, fields, and harvest to talk about people. When Jesus says the fields are ripe for harvest, what He means is that the people are ready and willing to receive His message.

This is not figurative or theoretical. He's talking about the woman and the townspeople she's bringing with her out to meet Him. The disciples would not have expected, and perhaps even wanted, this woman to respond to the gospel.

And yet here she was. The passage goes on to say that many Samaritans believed. Their eternal destiny was changed because of this woman. This is her legacy. We're still talking about her thousands of years after she's moved on.

Sowers and reapers do two different jobs. There's an entire season in between these two actions. They have the same goal—the harvest—but they operate at different times and with different functions.

This is part of what makes sowing into your future difficult. There's no celebration when you're sowing. Sometimes you feel like nothing is changing. Often you wonder if it's worth the time and energy. You may feel discouraged and even overcome with sadness. When you're in that place, it's not the time to give up. It's the time to double down and keep going.

Because when the harvest comes in, we celebrate together.

SEEDS: TOMORROW STARTS TODAY

WEEK SIX

JOHN 4:35-38

[35] "Don't you have a saying, 'It's still four months until harvest'? I tell you, open your eyes and look at the fields! They are ripe for harvest. [36] Even now the one who reaps draws a wage and harvests a crop for eternal life, so that the sower and the reaper may be glad together. [37] Thus the saying 'One sows and another reaps' is true. [38] I sent you to reap what you have not worked for. Others have done the hard work, and you have reaped the benefits of their labor."

CONTEXT

One of Jesus' most well-known encounters takes place in John 4. He's been down in Judea and now He's heading back up to Galilee. But instead of following the common cultural practice of going around Samaria, He went and stopped at a well where He talked to a woman with a questionable reputation.

The Jews despised Samaritans. While it was true the Samaritans' ancestors had abandoned the God of the Bible for foreign gods and unrighteous lifestyles, Jesus was about to challenge the Jews' self-righteous, prejudiced attitudes with a better way.

Jesus tells the woman to go get her husband, and when she tells Him she doesn't have one, He responds by saying she's actually had five plus the guy she's currently living with.

Understandably, the woman panics. She can't figure out how Jesus knows all this, and now she's even more embarrassed and feels unworthy to be talking to this Jewish man.

Instead of condemning her, Jesus invites her into an eternal relationship with the living God—the very thing she had been waiting and hoping for. She's so overcome with emotion that she runs back to the town to get everyone she knows to come and meet Jesus.

The disciples show up and they have no clue what Jesus is up to. They're inconvenienced and upset that they're in Samaria—and they can't believe He's talking to this woman. They're hungry and want to leave.

Jesus takes a moment to teach them about seeds, the Kingdom, and leaving a legacy.

WEEK SIX

Legacy is bigger than statues, monuments, or trophies we build to honor ourselves. No one cares for their own monument after they're gone. It's impossible. No one can defend their honor or worth after they've died. Only other people can do this for you.

Unfortunately, the human approach has prioritized the wrong things from the beginning of time. Jesus' Kingdom operates by a different standard.

His approach always comes back to participating in God's mission to bring the message of Jesus to the world through loving and serving people.

That legacy is eternal; it lasts forever. And it's what we really care about.

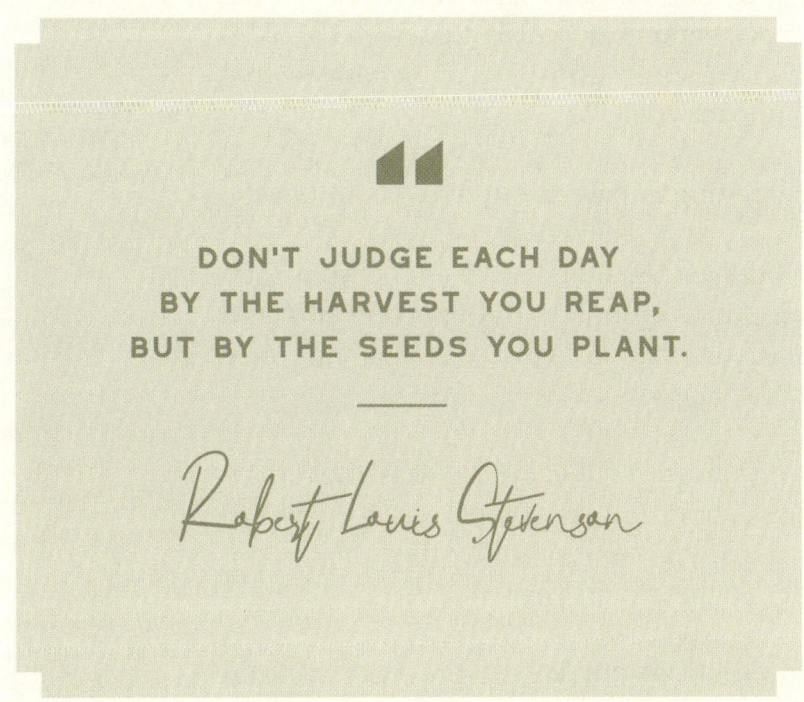

> DON'T JUDGE EACH DAY
> BY THE HARVEST YOU REAP,
> BUT BY THE SEEDS YOU PLANT.
>
> — *Robert Louis Stevenson*

SEEDS: TOMORROW STARTS TODAY

CONCEPT

The life cycle of a seed can vary greatly—some go into the ground, fail to germinate, and disappear.

Others take root, become a seedling, endure through difficult seasons, and continue to reproduce for many seasons providing an ongoing harvest.

The difference can be measured in days, months, years, and even centuries. The same is true of our lives, our words, our beliefs, and our actions.

If you stopped and carefully thought about it, I'm sure you could remember words that were spoken to you many years ago—positive or negative—that continue to impact your life.

The ongoing, lasting impact of our lives is our legacy.

Our legacy outlives us. Our legacy is the sum total of the contributions we made through our gifts and resources into the people who will live on once we're gone.

Jesus was very aware of legacy. He was moved by people whose actions inspired others and were worth remembering many generations after they moved on. (for example, Matthew 26:13).

Failing to think about our legacy prevents us from prioritizing the things that truly matter.

MATTHEW 26:13

"TRULY I TELL YOU, WHEREVER THIS GOSPEL IS PREACHED THROUGHOUT THE WORLD, WHAT SHE HAS DONE WILL ALSO BE TOLD, IN MEMORY OF HER."

WEEK SIX

THOSE WHO GO OUT WEEPING, CARRYING SEED TO SOW, WILL RETURN WITH SONGS OF JOY, CARRYING SHEAVES WITH THEM.
PSALM 126:6

SEEDS: TOMORROW STARTS TODAY

WEEK FIVE

4   Read 2 Corinthians 9:7. Would you describe yourself as a cheerful giver? Why or why not?

5   Read 2 Corinthians 9:10. According to this verse, what does God supply for us? How is that significant?

6   Read 2 Corinthians 9:11. According to this verse, why does God enrich and bless us?

7   Have you ever thought, "Later in life, when I have more, I plan on being more generous"? What's wrong with that way of thinking?

8   Are you afraid of not having enough? Or are you consistently looking for opportunities to be generous and invest in others? How can you grow in this area?

1. Read Luke 6:43-45. According to these verses, how can you tell a person's character?

2. Whatever is in a person's heart will eventually come out. Have you ever been shocked at what came out of your heart before—revealed by your words or actions? What was it, and what did you do about it?

3. Read 2 Corinthians 9:6. How does this verse apply to generosity? How could this verse apply to other areas of life like forgiveness, obedience, love, kindness, etc.?

SEEDS: TOMORROW STARTS TODAY

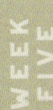
WEEK FIVE

> HE WHO SUPPLIES SEED TO THE SOWER AND BREAD FOR FOOD WILL SUPPLY AND MULTIPLY YOUR SEED FOR SOWING AND INCREASE THE HARVEST OF YOUR RIGHTEOUSNESS.
>
> 2 CORINTHIANS 9:10 (ESV)

SEEDS: TOMORROW STARTS TODAY

WHAT DO I DO WITH THIS?

WEEK FIVE

**When God asks you to do something,
do you feel obligated, or
is your first response to obey?**

If you find yourself constantly
dragging your feet and looking for a way out,
this is a good sign there's an issue in your heart.

**A persistent obedience problem
is less about understanding information
and more about loving something more than God.**

Are you afraid of not having enough?
Or are you consistently looking for
opportunities to be generous and invest in others?

In this passage, Paul tells the people to give what they've determined in their hearts to do, not because they're being forced or coerced but because they genuinely want to. It's so simple: "God loves a cheerful giver."

Paul tells them God is so generous Himself that He always makes a way for every one of His people to have enough so they can be ready to contribute to every good work they come across.

Look at this incredible insight. Paul says that the same God who gives you seed to sow and bread for food will supply and multiply your seed for sowing and increase your harvest of righteousness.

It's easy to miss the significance of this. Remember the Parable of the Sower. **Good seed is always multiplied from 30 to 60 to even 100 times what we planted.**

We don't eat seed and we don't plant bread. Seeds are our words, our thoughts, our actions, and our financial resources. We plant them; we don't eat them. When we're generous with our seed, not only do we have enough to provide for ourselves and our loved ones, but we can also expect our resources to be multiplied so we can always be generous and participate with what God's doing.

It's like there's this other container of seed God has available for those who trust Him enough to give it away. Have you ever met someone who said, "Later in life, when I have more, I plan on being more generous?" We all have. Most of us have said it ourselves.

But the truth is, on our own, we don't magically wake up generous one day. We become more and more of who we've been all along. When we get more, our desires and our expenses multiply too!

Whether we're talking about generosity, our ability to forgive others, our willingness to obey God, our understanding of His Word, or our willingness to respond in faith, what comes out of our heart will be multiplied in our lives.

SEEDS: TOMORROW STARTS TODAY

WEEK FIVE

2 CORINTHIANS 9:6-11 (ESV)

⁶ The point is this: whoever sows sparingly will also reap sparingly, and whoever sows bountifully will also reap bountifully. ⁷ Each one must give as he has decided in his heart, not reluctantly or under compulsion, for God loves a cheerful giver. ⁸ And God is able to make all grace abound to you, so that having all sufficiency in all things at all times, you may abound in every good work. ⁹ As it is written, "He has distributed freely, he has given to the poor; his righteousness endures forever."

¹⁰ He who supplies seed to the sower and bread for food will supply and multiply your seed for sowing and increase the harvest of your righteousness. ¹¹ You will be enriched in every way to be generous in every way, which through us will produce thanksgiving to God.

WEEK FIVE

WHAT DOES THIS MEAN FOR US TODAY?

Jesus makes it simple: You can tell the character of a person the same way you can tell the quality of a tree. What's coming out of their life? What they produce is a window into who they are.

You don't expect figs from thornbushes, and you don't expect generosity and forgiveness from someone who's consistently selfish.

It's important to remember what Jesus has already told us in His other parables. This process works inside out, not outside in. Good fruit doesn't make a bad tree good. What was already on the inside became visible.

In the same way, whatever is in a person's heart will eventually come out. If you listen to people (including yourself), they'll show you what kind of a person they are. Sooner or later, they'll make it clear.

What's on the inside will come out and will be multiplied.

This is why God repeatedly tells us He wants to give us a new heart (Ezekiel 36:26; Psalm 51:10; Hebrews 10:22).

He's not trying to manipulate and twist bad hearts into doing good things.

One area where we can see the difference between good and bad fruit is in our giving. Paul asks the people of the Corinthian church to join with him and to do their part to participate in what God's doing (2 Corinthians 9:6-11).

EZEKIEL 36:26

I WILL GIVE YOU A NEW HEART AND PUT A NEW SPIRIT IN YOU; I WILL REMOVE FROM YOU YOUR HEART OF STONE AND GIVE YOU A HEART OF FLESH.

PSALM 51:10

CREATE IN ME A PURE HEART, O GOD, AND RENEW A STEADFAST SPIRIT WITHIN ME.

HEBREWS 10:22

LET US DRAW NEAR TO GOD WITH A SINCERE HEART AND WITH THE FULL ASSURANCE THAT FAITH BRINGS, HAVING OUR HEARTS SPRINKLED TO CLEANSE US FROM A GUILTY CONSCIENCE AND HAVING OUR BODIES WASHED WITH PURE WATER.

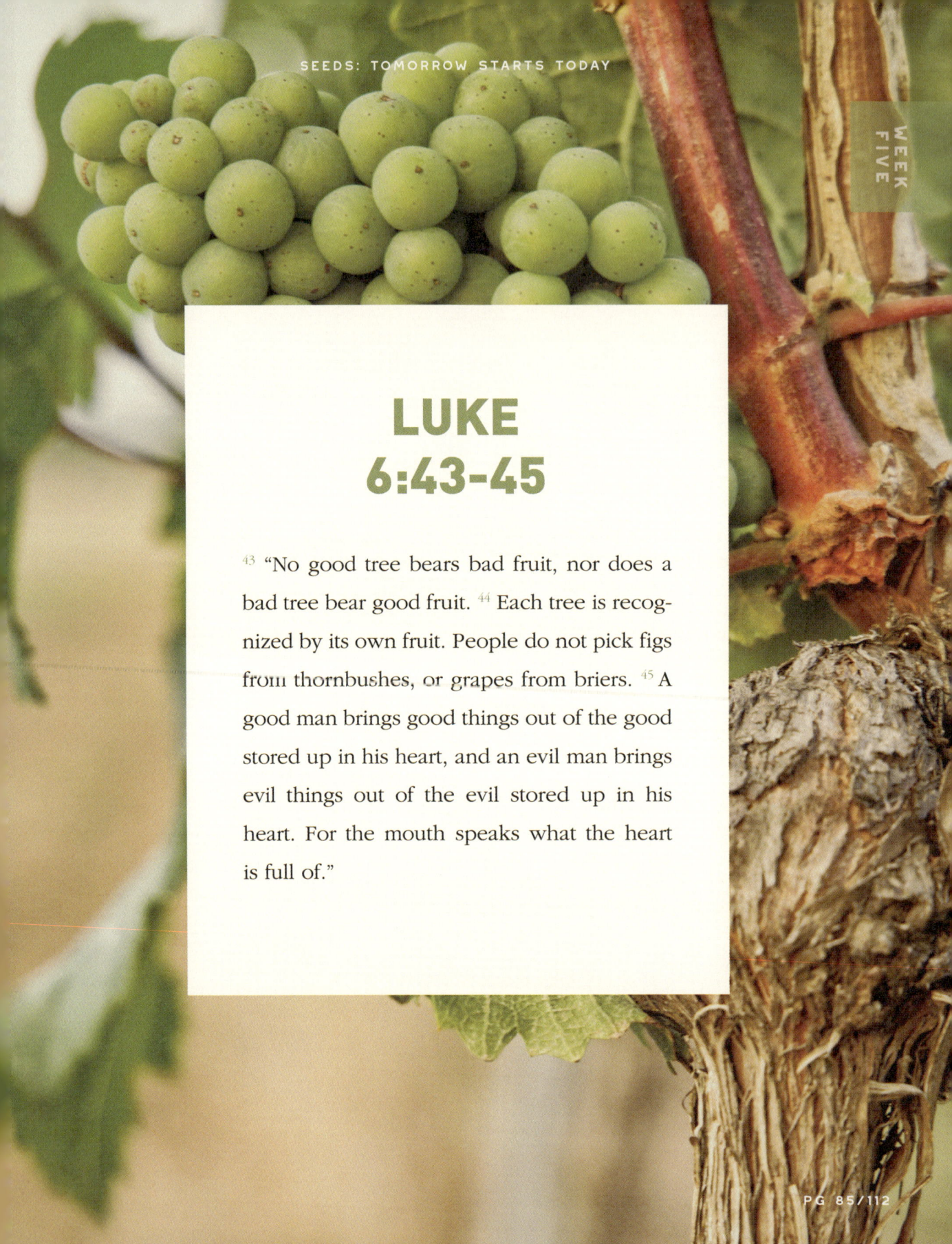

SEEDS: TOMORROW STARTS TODAY

WEEK FIVE

LUKE 6:43-45

⁴³ "No good tree bears bad fruit, nor does a bad tree bear good fruit. ⁴⁴ Each tree is recognized by its own fruit. People do not pick figs from thornbushes, or grapes from briers. ⁴⁵ A good man brings good things out of the good stored up in his heart, and an evil man brings evil things out of the evil stored up in his heart. For the mouth speaks what the heart is full of."

WEEK FIVE

CONTEXT

This is Luke's account of some of the early days of Jesus' ministry. Luke was a doctor and a companion of the apostle Paul who wrote both the third Gospel and the book of Acts.

At this point in the story, Jesus has just called His original disciples. He's walking with them, teaching them about God and life, and He's using daily moments like eating and healing the sick to demonstrate what He's talking about.

This passage in Luke 6 comes from his version of Jesus' most famous sermon, "The Sermon on the Mount." While it's not technically a parable, Jesus gives us a vivid metaphor directly related to seeds, trees, and fruit.

With enough time and care, a vast forest emerges from one tiny seed. That's the exponential power of multiplication.

There is a spruce tree in Sweden that scientists estimate to be more than 9,500 years old. This living, breathing testament to the wisdom of God has seen some things. Imagine the stories it could tell.

The very first Psalm compares the righteous person to a tree planted by water who does not wither but grows fruit in every season.

Jesus adds to this discussion and clarifies how we can understand people when we look at how trees work.

SEEDS: TOMORROW STARTS TODAY

WEEK FIVE

CONCEPT

Seeds are a small glimpse into the creative nature of God's character. He designed each part of His world to grow and expand—to reproduce after its own kind.

Everything that's healthy grows. It expands; it multiplies. This is how God set up the world.

You probably never thought about this, but did you know that after *God* and *people*, the Bible talks more about **trees** than anything else?

From Genesis to Revelation, and at many points in between, God uses the tree to teach us about Himself and how our world works. The Bible even says trees clap their hands (Isaiah 55:12) and sing in worship to God (1 Chronicles 16:33; Psalm 148:7a, 9).

If you plant one good seed in fertile soil with plenty of sunlight and rain, over time, you can grow a tree that blooms and produces fruit. This fruit will produce seeds, each of which carries the potential to reproduce after its own kind.

ISAIAH 55:12

YOU WILL GO OUT IN JOY AND BE LED FORTH IN PEACE; THE MOUNTAINS AND HILLS WILL BURST INTO SONG BEFORE YOU, AND ALL THE TREES OF THE FIELD WILL CLAP THEIR HANDS.

1 CHRONICLES 16:33

LET THE TREES OF THE FOREST SING,
LET THEM SING FOR JOY BEFORE THE LORD,
FOR HE COMES TO JUDGE THE EARTH.

PSALM 148:7a, 9

PRAISE THE LORD FROM THE EARTH . . . YOU MOUNTAINS AND ALL HILLS, FRUIT TREES AND ALL CEDARS.

HE WHO SUPPLIES SEED TO THE SOWER AND BREAD FOR FOOD WILL SUPPLY AND MULTIPLY YOUR SEED FOR SOWING AND INCREASE THE HARVEST OF YOUR RIGHTEOUSNESS. 2 CORINTHIANS 9:10 (ESV)

4   Have you ever thought about yourself as one of the weeds? How does this thought affect you? How does it change your understanding of who you are and who God is?

5   What is the only way for a weed to become wheat? How does this apply to you spiritually?

6   Read 1 Peter 1:23. What do you think it means to be "born again"?

7   On your spiritual journey, are you simply trying harder to become a better person, or have you received God's free gift of salvation? Explain.

8   Let's get practical. What areas in your life have changed since you have been saved? What is an area in your life that still needs to change or improve? How can God help you in this area?

1. Read Exodus 34:6. Why do you think this is the most repeated verse in the Bible? What does this verse tell you about God?

2. How does Exodus 34:6 affect your understanding of the parable of the weeds (Matthew 13:24-30, 36-43)?

3. According to this parable, who are the weeds, and where do they come from? (See verses 38-39.)

SEEDS: TOMORROW STARTS TODAY

WEEK FOUR

FOR YOU HAVE BEEN BORN AGAIN, NOT OF PERISHABLE SEED, BUT OF IMPERISHABLE, THROUGH THE LIVING AND ENDURING WORD OF GOD.

1 PETER 1:23

SEEDS: TOMORROW STARTS TODAY

WHAT DO I DO WITH THIS?

WEEK FOUR

Are you trying hard to prove to God
and yourself that you're good?
Or have you admitted your brokenness,
repented, and asked Him to make you new?

All of us wrestle with the ongoing presence
and existence of evil, but
we have to remember God's long-suffering
isn't weakness or negligence.

His patience isn't indifference—
it's His desire for all of His children
to come home to Him.

WEEK FOUR

Instead, we are transformed. We receive a new nature (2 Peter 1:4). We're born again (John 3:3).

Peter said that when we're born again to a new life, it's from a seed that will never perish. We're not part weed and part wheat trying our best to produce good fruit.

Paul contrasts the first human being Adam, who broke God's law and betrayed God's trust, with the second "Adam," who was born of the Spirit and lived in perfect obedience (Romans 5:12; 5:15).

The power of transformation is not our willpower and effort to be perfect and become a better version of Adam. Transformation comes through receiving the perfect obedience of the second Adam who gives His righteousness as a gift.

Jesus didn't come to help bad people get better. He came to bring people who were dead in sin back to life.

A weed who works really hard and tries to become wheat can't do it. For a while they may be able to fool the farmer. Eventually, the poison in the weed will come out.

The only way a weed can become wheat is to be re-created…to be born again. That's the power of transformation.

2 PETER 1:4

THROUGH THESE HE HAS GIVEN US HIS VERY GREAT AND PRECIOUS PROMISES, SO THAT THROUGH THEM YOU MAY PARTICIPATE IN THE DIVINE NATURE, HAVING ESCAPED THE CORRUPTION IN THE WORLD CAUSED BY EVIL DESIRES.

JOHN 3:3

JESUS REPLIED, "VERY TRULY I TELL YOU, NO ONE CAN SEE THE KINGDOM OF GOD UNLESS THEY ARE BORN AGAIN."

ROMANS 5:12

THEREFORE, JUST AS SIN ENTERED THE WORLD THROUGH ONE MAN, AND DEATH THROUGH SIN, AND IN THIS WAY DEATH CAME TO ALL PEOPLE, BECAUSE ALL SINNED.

ROMANS 5:15

BUT THE GIFT IS NOT LIKE THE TRESPASS. FOR IF THE MANY DIED BY THE TRESPASS OF THE ONE MAN, HOW MUCH MORE DID GOD'S GRACE AND THE GIFT THAT CAME BY THE GRACE OF THE ONE MAN, JESUS CHRIST, OVERFLOW TO THE MANY!

issue. AW Tozer once said, "What you think about when you think about God is the most important thing about you."

If you think you're a good person and the problem is everyone else, this makes you think God's allowing good people like you to suffer. He's failing to execute judgment on those who deserve it. He's not fulfilling His promises.

It's easy to think, "Yeah...let's get rid of all the weeds!" without realizing you are the weed.

In other words, you're good and God's bad. You might even say, you've become God.

But if you see yourself as imperfect, if you can own the mistakes you've made—especially to the people you love most—this patience on God's part doesn't look like weakness.

Your humility allows you to see it for what it truly is—*the compassion and grace of a God who is slow to anger, abounding in love and faithfulness.*

The only way to have a perfect relationship with a perfect God is to be perfect. We don't have it in us. All the willpower in the world can't make that happen.

Because this perfect God is so loving, He sent His perfect Son on our behalf, to live the life we should have but couldn't and to die the death in our place to close the gap between God and people.

Two of the primary leaders of the early church, Peter and Paul, understood the power of transformation better than anyone. It wasn't a theory to them; it was their life experience.

A genuine relationship with God was not something we could earn or produce out of our effort or willpower. It's a gift we receive by faith. We can't mentally ascend to it or grow through increased spiritual information.

WEEK FOUR

WHAT DOES THIS MEAN FOR US TODAY?

A parable like this one requires context. If we read it by itself, we can get the wrong picture in our minds.

Few people can tell you the most commonly repeated verse in the Bible. It's Exodus 34:6: "…The Lord, the Lord, the compassionate and gracious God, slow to anger, abounding in love and faithfulness…"

This is how God describes Himself. This is the God who allows weeds to grow alongside the wheat.

If we read the parable of the weeds with an arrogant attitude (God owes me something) or a fearful perspective (God's looking for a reason to punish me), we'll miss what this passage is all about.

Remember, the servants ask the right question: You sowed good seed, so where do the weeds come from?

The Bible's message is clear: we're *all* weeds. We come by it honestly. No one has to teach us to be selfish, to hurt others, to put our desires (even the ones that hurt us) above the needs of everyone else.

There's only One good seed, and He wasn't born of a man but the Spirit of God.

Even though it pains Him, God tolerates evil for the hope of those who will come home while He waits. **How does this change your perspective of God?**

This is the crux of the whole situation. This is the soil from which everything in our lives grows. We have to resolve this

MATTHEW 13:36-43

³⁶ Then he left the crowd and went into the house. His disciples came to him and said, "Explain to us the parable of the weeds in the field."

³⁷ He answered, "The one who sowed the good seed is the Son of Man. ³⁸ The field is the world, and the good seed stands for the people of the kingdom. The weeds are the people of the evil one, ³⁹ and the enemy who sows them is the devil. The harvest is the end of the age, and the harvesters are angels.

⁴⁰ "As the weeds are pulled up and burned in the fire, so it will be at the end of the age. ⁴¹ The Son of Man will send out his angels, and they will weed out of his kingdom everything that causes sin and all who do evil. ⁴² They will throw them into the blazing furnace, where there will be weeping and gnashing of teeth. ⁴³ Then the righteous will shine like the sun in the kingdom of their Father. Whoever has ears, let them hear."

MATTHEW 13:24-30

²⁴ Jesus told them another parable: "The kingdom of heaven is like a man who sowed good seed in his field. ²⁵ But while everyone was sleeping, his enemy came and sowed weeds among the wheat, and went away. ²⁶ When the wheat sprouted and formed heads, then the weeds also appeared.

²⁷ "The owner's servants came to him and said, 'Sir, didn't you sow good seed in your field? Where then did the weeds come from?'

²⁸ "'An enemy did this,' he replied.

"The servants asked him, 'Do you want us to go and pull them up?'

²⁹ "'No,' he answered, 'because while you are pulling the weeds, you may uproot the wheat with them. ³⁰ Let both grow together until the harvest. At that time I will tell the harvesters: First collect the weeds and tie them in bundles to be burned; then gather the wheat and bring it into my barn.'"

CONTEXT

Jesus has officially turned up the heat.

He's not only talking about seeds, now He starts talking about letting everything grow together until it's time to gather and separate the harvest. One pile to be put in His barn and one pile to be burned.

If this sounds unnerving, it's all by design. Jesus has gone from talking about our day-to-day experience to directly addressing our ultimate destiny. He's raised the stakes.

He's not doing this to scare us but to inspire us into a deeper relationship with Him.

SEEDS: TOMORROW STARTS TODAY

WEEK FOUR

FOR YOU HAVE BEEN BORN AGAIN, NOT OF PERISHABLE SEED, BUT OF IMPERISHABLE, THROUGH THE LIVING AND ENDURING WORD OF GOD. 1 PETER 1:23

CONCEPT

When winter turns to spring, most varieties of grass change from yellow to a shade of green. Depending on their species and proximity to sunlight and rain, this transformation happens at different speeds.

Often there are bright patches of green that change color more quickly and dramatically. It looks so healthy and appealing. But any landscaper or gardener will tell you that this is not good. To the untrained eye it looks pleasing, but before long the truth will become clear. This isn't grass—it's weeds.

Failing to deal with the weeds threatens the grass. You can't nurture weeds into becoming grass. The only way to solve the issue is to pull the weeds and plant good seed.

Jesus is going to show us that the same is true with people.

4. What does Mark's relationship with Peter show you about the power of spiritual momentum in Mark's life?

5. Scattering seed is the first step in God's process for change. The seed can be your thoughts, attitudes, actions, or words. What seeds (thoughts, attitudes, actions, or words) are you planting in your life? Are they good or bad? Be specific.

6. What is your role and God's role in the growth process? What are you responsible for, and what is He?

7. How is the biblical principle of sowing seed different from the concept of karma?

8. Let's get practical. Think of an area in your life that you want to see change. Now, what is your part—what can you do to help bring about the change? What is God's part? Whose part is more important?

1. When have you felt the power of momentum before? What was it like? (Don't think about spiritual momentum right now; focus on momentum in general.)

2. Have you ever considered that your life can gain spiritual momentum? What do you think spiritual momentum looks like?

3. It's interesting to think that Mark once had a rocky relationship with the apostle Paul that ended with them going separate ways. Then Peter took him under his wing and gave him a second chance. What does this show you about the "realness" of the people in the Bible?

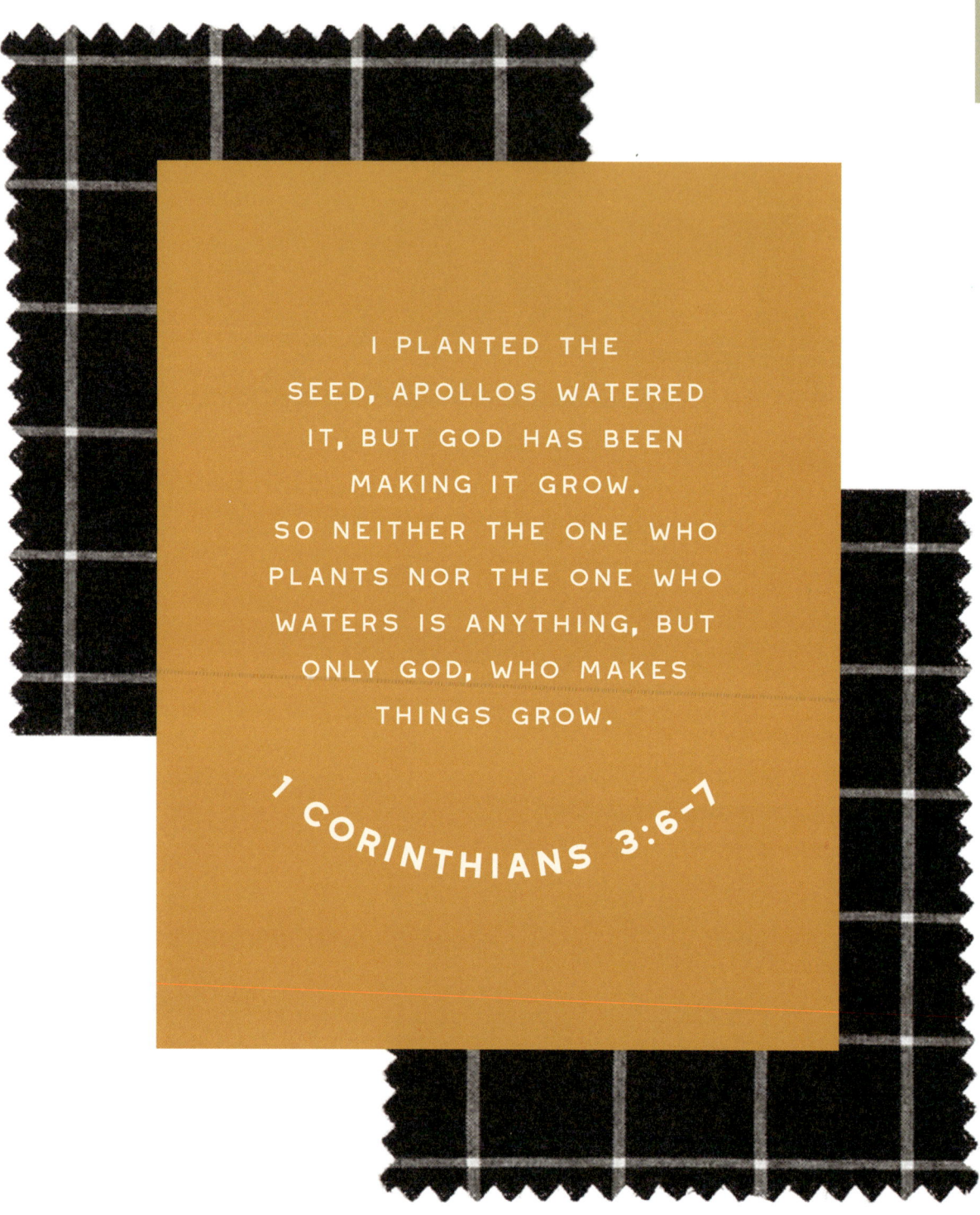

SEEDS: TOMORROW STARTS TODAY

WEEK THREE

WHAT DO I DO WITH THIS?

When something bad happens in your life, do you look for someone to blame?

Do you view it as the judgment of God? Do you believe He's looking for ways to punish you?

When something good happens, are you quick to take credit?

Are you tempted to make yourself feel better by comparing yourself to others who have less than you do?

Neither of these approaches help us in the long term. Instead, we need to focus on ourselves and take responsibility for the seed we're planting.

Are you focused on doing your part, while you trust in faith that God will do what only He can do?

We can control our thoughts, our words, and our actions. When they align with God and His Word, we can trust that eventually we'll receive what God has for us. He's the source of momentum. He's better than karma. He has both grace and mercy for our lives.

The grace of God is a gift. We don't earn it. We don't deserve it. We don't get it as a result of our hard work and planting. In more ways than we understand or recognize, everything good in our lives comes through the grace of God.

The mercy of God is also a gift. Mercy means we've been spared from the punishment or consequences we've earned.

Mercy and grace are so much better than karma.

Karma says you get what you earn. Because we're so determined to control our lives, we think if we do good, we get good, and if we do bad, we get bad.

While this can often be true, God created the world with more nuance, subtlety, and mystery than this. As a loving Father, He's deeply invested in helping us move far beyond what we can earn in order to enjoy the goodness that's only possible in and through Him.

We can't earn it. That's His part. But we can participate by doing our part. And when we understand this, we experience the momentum of the grace and mercy of God.

SEEDS: TOMORROW STARTS TODAY

WEEK THREE

STEP THREE: GROWTH PRODUCES HARVEST. Jesus' audience would have recognized the metaphor of the sickle and the harvest in verse 29 as symbols of the final judgment when God comes to evaluate what we've done with what we've been given.

In his letter to the church in Corinth, Paul picks up on this concept (1 Corinthians 3:6-7). In that church, there was both good and bad seed. They were trying to figure out who gets the credit or the blame. They wanted to know if their outcomes were tied to their actions or their mentors. They didn't want to follow the process.

Paul wanted them to see that growth always comes back to our relationship with God. We all plant seed. Other people who lead and serve us help water those seeds. But only God makes things grow.

Momentum comes from leaning into God's wisdom and His principles. It doesn't always come immediately, but if we keep focused on God and His Word, eventually we'll discover the momentum we're looking for and we'll grow—even when we can't explain how.

This can be hard for us, but this approach is so much better. The way God designs us to grow causes us to trust Him. We can't guarantee outcomes.

Clearly there is a principle of sowing and reaping in the Bible. But it's even better than this. If we only received what we sowed, we'd miss out on two of the biggest gifts God gives us.

1 CORINTHIANS 3:6-7

6 I PLANTED THE SEED, APOLLOS WATERED IT, BUT GOD HAS BEEN MAKING IT GROW. 7 SO NEITHER THE ONE WHO PLANTS NOR THE ONE WHO WATERS IS ANYTHING, BUT ONLY GOD, WHO MAKES THINGS GROW.

WHAT DOES THIS MEAN FOR US TODAY?

STEP ONE: GET THE SEED ON THE GROUND. You can't skip this step. You'll never have momentum if you're not scattering seed.

You have to do your part. You choose your thoughts. You choose your attitudes. You choose whether or not to obey. You choose the words you speak. No one else can do it for you.

Each of these actions are seeds we put in the ground. But once they've been scattered, they go to work. At this point, no matter what we've done, they start to sprout and grow.

If we go all the way back to Genesis chapter 1, we see this principle of participation. God sets up His good world, puts it in motion, and then invites us into the process. And then He sits back to watch what we do with what He's given us.

STEP TWO: GOD CAUSES THE GROWTH. We don't have control or complete understanding of how the process works. We can't explain all the outcomes. But because this is God's process, He watches over it and ensures it accomplishes His purposes and plan.

Verse 28 starts with a funny little phrase, "All by itself the soil produces grain…" We know there's more to it than that, but we also know the part that we control is small. *Our job is not to make things grow; our job is to be very aware of what we're planting.*

We want good seed going in the ground to produce a great harvest.

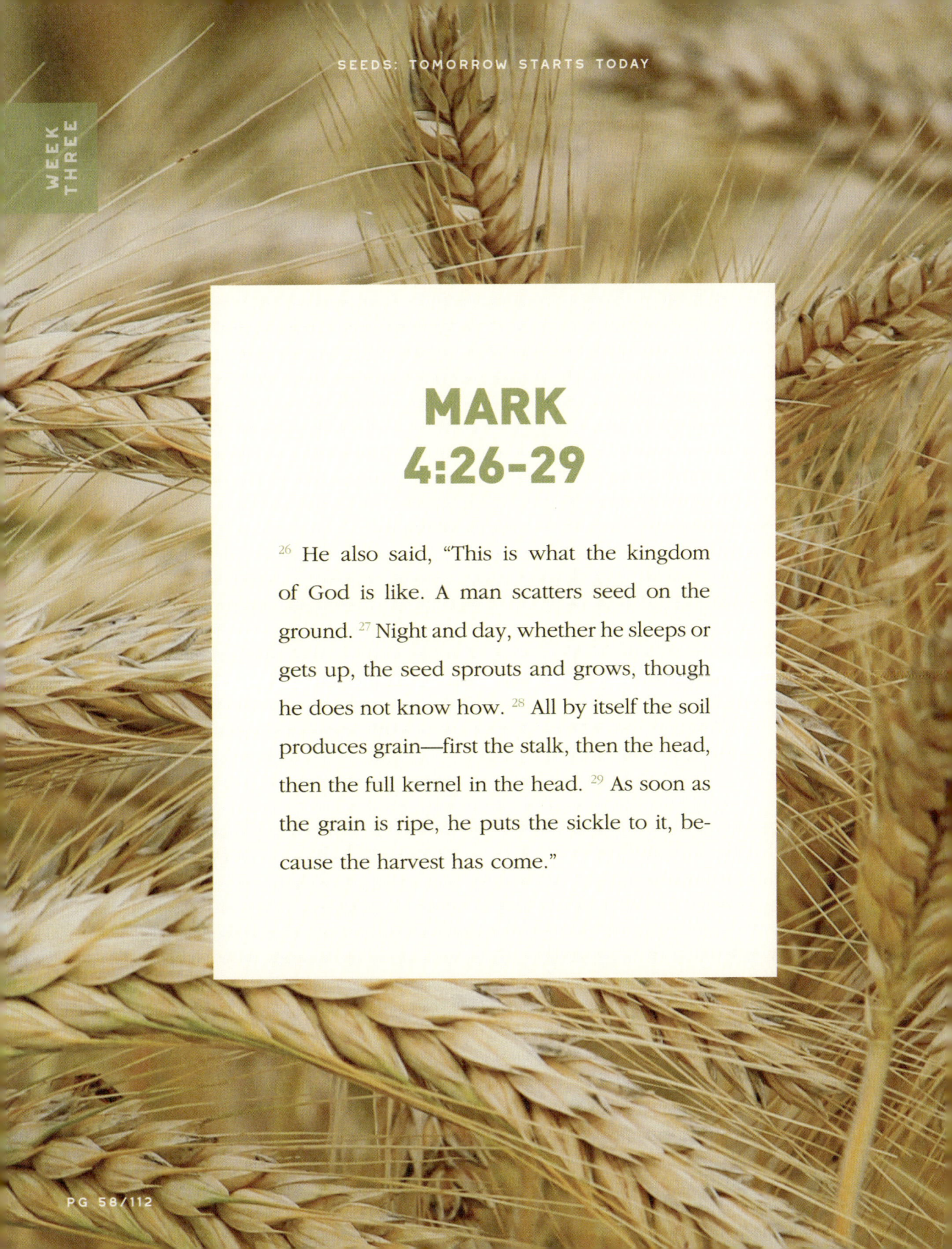

WEEK THREE

SEEDS: TOMORROW STARTS TODAY

MARK 4:26-29

²⁶ He also said, "This is what the kingdom of God is like. A man scatters seed on the ground. ²⁷ Night and day, whether he sleeps or gets up, the seed sprouts and grows, though he does not know how. ²⁸ All by itself the soil produces grain—first the stalk, then the head, then the full kernel in the head. ²⁹ As soon as the grain is ripe, he puts the sickle to it, because the harvest has come."

CONTEXT

Jesus tells a short parable about this concept. It's only four verses long and it only shows up in the Gospel of Mark. None of the other Gospels include it.

The parable is tucked in between two parables we've already looked at: The Parable of the Sower and The Parable of the Mustard Seed.

History tells us that the Gospel of Mark comes directly from the life experience of the disciple Peter. He was close to Jesus. He is featured prominently in all the big moments.

Mark started as a companion of the apostle Paul, but Paul was frustrated with Mark's immaturity and moved on. Peter took Mark under his wing and gave him another chance. Later in life, under the inspiration of the Holy Spirit, Mark wrote down this Gospel.

It's interesting that only Peter included this story. The parable matches his personality. Peter was impulsive and always hurrying to the next thing. His personality is reflected in the book of Mark, which is also written in a fast-paced style. This short parable also moves quickly but carries a lot of weight (Mark 4:26-29).

CONCEPT

Life is busy. It moves fast. There are many days where it feels like simply keeping up is a challenging goal.

In those moments, how do you slow the tide of difficult tasks long enough to prioritize the things that really matter? It's not easy.

What we really want is to lean into the other seasons—those rare and precious moments where it seems like one good thing after another comes our way. We search for a reason to explain why we feel the wind at our backs.

We know it's irrational, but we think it's because we're starting the day the same way. Maybe it's our lucky shirt. Whatever it is, we want to do whatever it takes to keep it going.

We're grasping to control or explain things we don't understand.

Science has a term for this, and now we use it in our everyday lives: *momentum*.

Momentum is when things are all moving quickly in the same direction. We're all searching for it. Once we have it, we do whatever it takes to keep it.

Spiritual momentum comes from understanding the difference between your part and God's part. **You focus on what He asks you to do while you trust Him to do what only He can do.**

This makes all the difference.

4. How does the parable of the mustard seed illustrate the expansion of God's Kingdom on earth?

5. How does the parable of the mustard seed illustrate the role of faith in the life of the believer?

6. Have you ever had to trust God for something big before? What happened?

7. If you had to rate your level of faith in God on a scale of 1-10, how would you rate yourself? Explain.

8. Is there something big you're trusting God to do right now? What is it, and what is something you can do to trust God more in this situation?

1   How would you describe faith—what is it? What is it not?

2   How is faith relational?

3   Why is faith necessary for the changes you want to see happen in your life?

SEEDS: TOMORROW STARTS TODAY

WEEK TWO

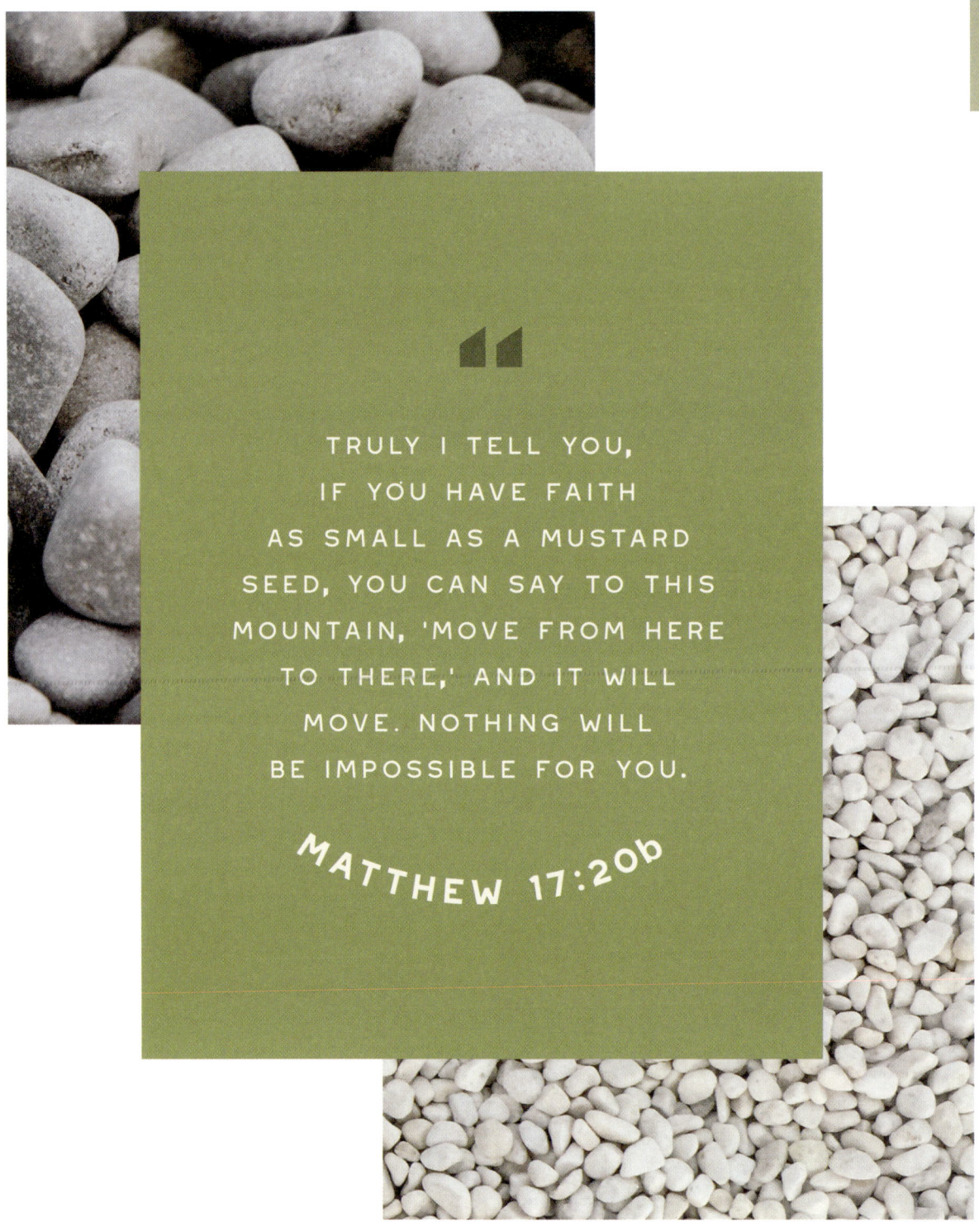

> "
>
> TRULY I TELL YOU, IF YOU HAVE FAITH AS SMALL AS A MUSTARD SEED, YOU CAN SAY TO THIS MOUNTAIN, 'MOVE FROM HERE TO THERE,' AND IT WILL MOVE. NOTHING WILL BE IMPOSSIBLE FOR YOU.
>
> MATTHEW 17:20b

SEEDS: TOMORROW STARTS TODAY

WEEK TWO

WHAT DO I DO WITH THIS?

Do you have this kind of faith? What are you doing today to build the faith you will need tomorrow?

When you look at your tomorrow—when you think about where you'd like to be a year from now—do you have faith to see it become a reality?

Faith is a conviction and a promise that comes from hearing God's Word. Write down several of the faith scriptures listed on page 45, and put them where you will see them on a daily basis—on your bathroom mirror, on the dashboard of your car, or on the back of your phone.

What everyone considered small would quickly become large right before their eyes. This is how the Kingdom of God works.

In Matthew 17, Jesus returns to this concept.

He takes His three closest disciples up on the mountain to hear from God. When they return to the rest of the disciples, there's a big crowd of people gathered around them. The other disciples are freaking out because they've been praying for a boy who's been traumatized by evil spirits. The boy's dad comes up to Jesus and throws himself at His feet and cries out for mercy.

Jesus is frustrated with the inability of the disciples to help this man and his son. He prays for the boy, and he's immediately healed. When they ask Jesus why they couldn't do it, He tells them it's because they have so little faith.

He tells them if they had faith even as small as a mustard seed, nothing would be impossible for them. They could move mountains—which was an ancient expression used to describe supernatural power.

Jesus' point is simple. Faith is personal, but it's not private. It's not internal. It's not cerebral. It impacts how we live. It impacts our circumstances.

Faith may start small, but it always grows until everyone who comes around it can see it. Faith grows. Faith changes things.

WHAT DOES THIS MEAN FOR US TODAY?

You may wonder why Matthew uses this phrase, "the kingdom of heaven."

In most cases, Matthew uses the phrase "kingdom of heaven" instead of the phrase, "Kingdom of God," found in Mark, Luke, and John. Bible scholars believe Matthew is not referring to heaven or some other place but is opting for this expression as a "circumlocution"—a roundabout way of talking about the Kingdom of God without using the name God.

Of the four Gospels, Matthew is most directly addressed to a Jewish audience, and the most pious Jews believed God's name was so holy it was not meant to be used casually. Matthew is avoiding repeated use of God's name out of consideration for this crowd.

The mustard seed is not the smallest seed in the world (there's a rain forest orchid that produces microscopic seeds), but it was the smallest seed in their world.

Jesus' point remains: From this tiny seed would grow a mustard tree which we might describe as a bush, but they would regularly grow between eight and twelve feet tall. At that size, they would be very large for a garden and many birds could rest on their branches.

SEEDS: TOMORROW STARTS TODAY

WEEK TWO

MATTHEW 13:31-32

³¹ He told them another parable: "The kingdom of heaven is like a mustard seed, which a man took and planted in his field. ³² Though it is the smallest of all seeds, yet when it grows, it is the largest of garden plants and becomes a tree, so that the birds come and perch in its branches."

CONTEXT

Matthew chapter 13 includes seven different parables from Jesus. The longest of these parables is one we've already looked at, "The Parable of the Sower." Of the seven parables, three of them deal directly with seeds. In this guide, we'll study all three.

In keeping with His strategy of giving a relational invitation more than spiritual information, Jesus keeps giving parables to the people without explanations. He piles one after another. You get the sense the people were looking back at Him with a puzzled sense of confusion. What did it mean?

We know they felt this way because the disciples kept asking for extra help. And because of their willingness to ask, Jesus' willingness to answer, and the wisdom of God in compiling Scripture, we have access to the wisdom of God.

Jesus told His disciples that the great prophets and righteous people from previous generations longed for this insight without ever receiving it. This should fill our hearts with gratitude.

CONCEPT

Potential, process, and resistance all include uncertainty. We hope we'll get through the resistance to the promise on the other side… but we have to wait and see. We're looking for something to hold on to.

We need a confidence bigger than our fear and a trust deeper than our circumstances. The Bible calls this "faith."

If tomorrow starts today, then the bridge between the two is faith.

Faith is a promise (Romans 4:20). It's a conviction of things we can't see (Hebrews 11:1), and with patience, it's the way we receive what God has promised (Hebrews 6:12). Faith comes from hearing the Word (Romans 10:17) and without faith, it's impossible to come to God or to please Him (Hebrews 11:6).

Faith is not a belief system; faith is not spiritual information; faith is not religious duty. Faith is relational—both in how we receive it and where we put it. Faith is the deep, childlike trust a person puts in God.

Faith is not something we muster up on our own—it's a gift we receive from God.

We can't talk about seeds without talking about faith.

ROMANS 4:20

YET HE DID NOT WAVER THROUGH UNBELIEF REGARDING THE PROMISE OF GOD, BUT WAS STRENGTHENED IN HIS FAITH AND GAVE GLORY TO GOD.

HEBREWS 11:1

NOW FAITH IS CONFIDENCE IN WHAT WE HOPE FOR AND ASSURANCE ABOUT WHAT WE DO NOT SEE.

HEBREWS 6:12

WE DO NOT WANT YOU TO BECOME LAZY, BUT TO IMITATE THOSE WHO THROUGH FAITH AND PATIENCE INHERIT WHAT HAS BEEN PROMISED.

ROMANS 10:17

CONSEQUENTLY, FAITH COMES FROM HEARING THE MESSAGE, AND THE MESSAGE IS HEARD THROUGH THE WORD ABOUT CHRIST.

HEBREWS 11:6

AND WITHOUT FAITH IT IS IMPOSSIBLE TO PLEASE GOD, BECAUSE ANYONE WHO COMES TO HIM MUST BELIEVE THAT HE EXISTS AND THAT HE REWARDS THOSE WHO EARNESTLY SEEK HIM.

WEEK TWO

"TRULY I TELL YOU, IF YOU HAVE FAITH AS SMALL AS A MUSTARD SEED, YOU CAN SAY TO THIS MOUNTAIN, 'MOVE FROM HERE TO THERE,' AND IT WILL MOVE. NOTHING WILL BE IMPOSSIBLE FOR YOU." MATTHEW 17:20b

4. Read Matthew 13:19. Have you ever seen the enemy steal the truth of God's Word from someone before, or has it happened to you? Explain.

5. Read Matthew 13:20-21. The seed that fell on rocky ground sprang up quickly but fell away because it had no root. Have you ever known someone like that? Who is it, and why?

6. Read Matthew 13:22. How do the worries of life and the deceitfulness of wealth choke out God's Word?

7. Which person in the parable do you most identify with and why?

8. Read Matthew 13:23. How can we receive God's Word and produce 30, 60, and 100 times what was planted? Try to be specific (practical) in your answer.

Take a few moments to go over the discussion questions below, so you can talk about them with your Small Group.

1. God's process for growth and change is always slow and takes time. How does our modern culture fight against God's process?

2. How do you typically handle adversity or resistance—when things don't happen the way you want or as fast as you want?

3. How does God want us to handle adversity and resistance?

SEEDS: TOMORROW STARTS TODAY

WEEK ONE

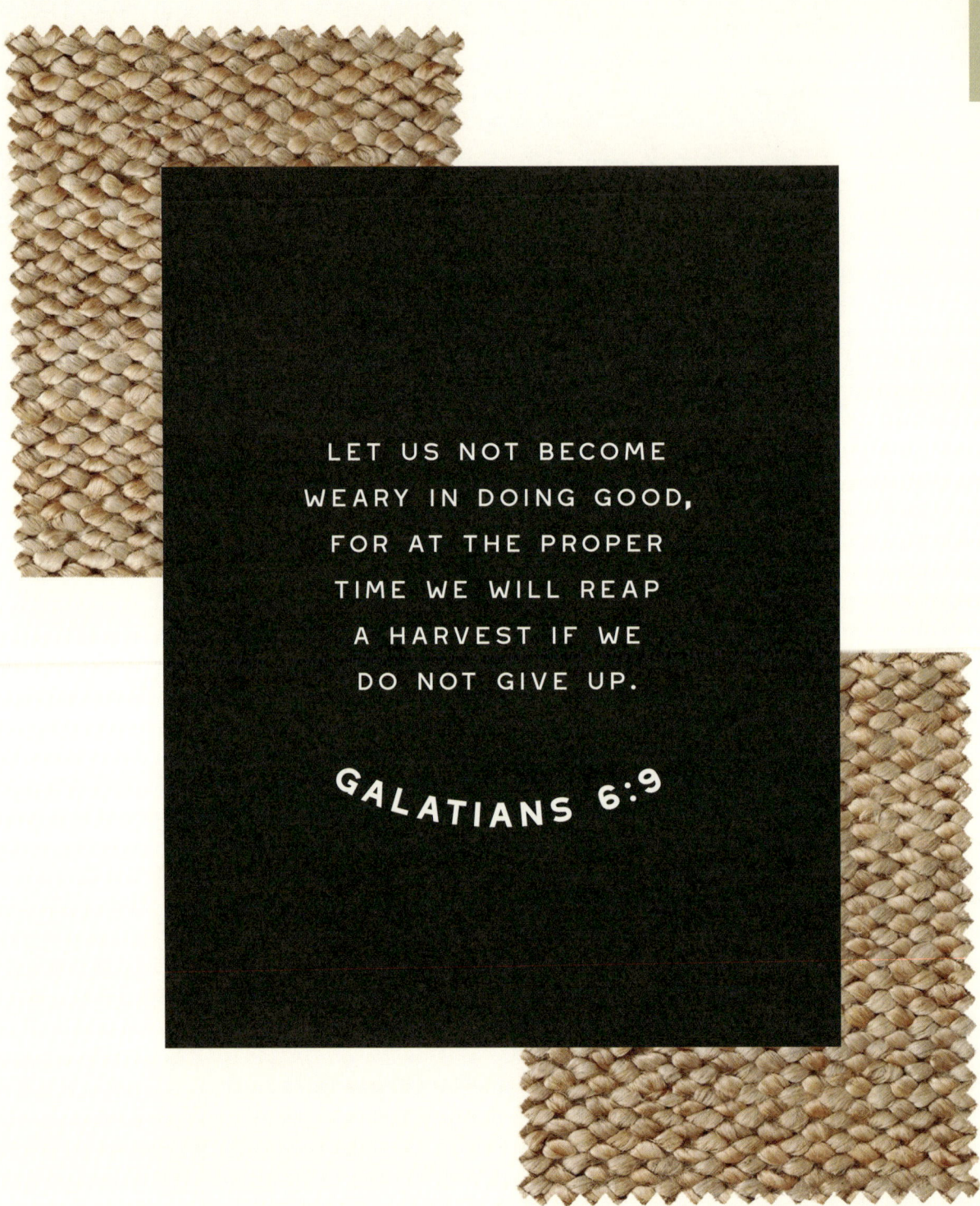

LET US NOT BECOME
WEARY IN DOING GOOD,
FOR AT THE PROPER
TIME WE WILL REAP
A HARVEST IF WE
DO NOT GIVE UP.

GALATIANS 6:9

SEEDS: TOMORROW STARTS TODAY

WEEK ONE

WHAT DO I DO WITH THIS?

What happens when you meet resistance?

When you look forward into this year, and you consider where you want to be a year from now, how will you respond to the challenges you face?

WHAT WILL YOU DO WHEN YOU FEEL DISCOURAGED AND YOU DON'T UNDERSTAND WHAT GOD'S ASKING YOU TO DO?

HOW WILL YOU RESPOND WHEN YOU FEEL LIKE YOU WANT TO QUIT?

WHERE WILL YOU TURN WHEN YOU'RE CHOKED BY WORRY?

It's interesting to note these things come "…because of the word…" Whenever God speaks to us, there will always be resistance. The temptation is often to be surprised when other people don't support or encourage you when God speaks to you. Jesus said we shouldn't be surprised. It's part of the process.

The seed falling among the thorns represents someone who hears the message, but the worries of life and the deceptive power of wealth choke out the word and make it unfruitful. In another passage, Jesus reassured the people not to worry because God knows what they need. If we're always worried, it's hard for us to hold on to God's Word. Worry has a way of choking everything else out.

In case it's not clear, each of these three challenges can and do happen to all of us. This is why Jesus is teaching on this subject. He knows us. He knows what we go through.

> **We all can be deceived in our thoughts,
> our attitudes, and our actions.
> We all can be tempted to quit
> when we face trouble and persecution.
> And we all can be overcome with worry.**

But we all can be the good seed. This is anyone who hears the word, receives it, applies it, and produces a crop 30, 60, or 100 times what was invested. This idea of producing a crop or bearing fruit means the things of the Kingdom—faith, joy, hope, forgiveness, compassion, obedience—pop up all over our lives.

SEEDS: TOMORROW STARTS TODAY

WHAT DOES THIS MEAN FOR US TODAY?

Don't you love when Jesus says, "Listen to what this means…" We all want this kind of relationship with God. This is what Jesus makes possible—He helps us make sense of life.

Just to be clear, this passage applies to every area of our lives. It's a window into how we grow and change. But it's important to remember the primary application of this parable is how people hear and receive the message of the gospel.

Jesus explains what He means when He talks about seed falling on the path. When anyone hears the message about the Kingdom and doesn't understand, the evil one comes and snatches away what was sown.

The "evil one" includes the person of Satan, his forces, and his system. In other words, it's not a dramatic encounter where they see the evil one and are afraid. It's happening without them being aware. They're buying into a system that promotes other attitudes, values other objectives, and lies about the inherent value of God and His Kingdom.

The seed falling on the rocky ground represents someone who hears the word, is immediately excited, but gives up after a short time because of trouble or persecution.

SEEDS: TOMORROW STARTS TODAY

WEEK ONE

MATTHEW 13:18-23

[18] "Listen then to what the parable of the sower means: [19] When anyone hears the message about the kingdom and does not understand it, the evil one comes and snatches away what was sown in their heart. This is the seed sown along the path. [20] The seed falling on rocky ground refers to someone who hears the word and at once receives it with joy. [21] But since they have no root, they last only a short time. When trouble or persecution comes because of the word, they quickly fall away.

[22] The seed falling among the thorns refers to someone who hears the word, but the worries of this life and the deceitfulness of wealth choke the word, making it unfruitful. [23] But the seed falling on good soil refers to someone who hears the word and understands it. This is the one who produces a crop, yielding a hundred, sixty or thirty times what was sown."

CONTEXT

When we first looked at "The Parable of the Sower," Jesus told a short story about a farmer who threw seed out on the field. The seed fell in a variety of places, but the good seed returned a harvest of 30, 60, or 100 times what was planted.

Instead of explaining what He meant, Jesus basically says, "Whoever really wants to know will keep searching." More than presenting information, Jesus gives an invitation to an ongoing relationship.

This is a key component of Jesus' approach to ministry. He didn't always say this so clearly, but it's always there in His interactions. He doesn't expect people to understand everything, but He does want them to keep following, even when they don't get it. This was true then, but it's also true for us today.

The disciples don't understand, so they ask Jesus why He was being so mysterious. He tells them this was God's plan. He shows them a prophetic Old Testament passage that reveals this pattern (Matthew 13:10-17).

The problem isn't a lack of desire on God's part to speak to His people. The real problem is the unwillingness of the people to listen, to lean in, to prioritize the voice of the Lord, and to obey what He asks them to do. This is a big theme in the Bible.

Now Jesus is going to explain why this continues to happen (Matthew 13:18-23).

MATTHEW 13:10-17

10 THE DISCIPLES CAME TO HIM AND ASKED, "WHY DO YOU SPEAK TO THE PEOPLE IN PARABLES?" 11 HE REPLIED, "BECAUSE THE KNOWLEDGE OF THE SECRETS OF THE KINGDOM OF HEAVEN HAS BEEN GIVEN TO YOU, BUT NOT TO THEM. 12 WHOEVER HAS WILL BE GIVEN MORE, AND THEY WILL HAVE AN ABUNDANCE. WHOEVER DOES NOT HAVE, EVEN WHAT THEY HAVE WILL BE TAKEN FROM THEM. 13 THIS IS WHY I SPEAK TO THEM IN PARABLES: 'THOUGH SEEING, THEY DO NOT SEE; THOUGH HEARING, THEY DO NOT HEAR OR UNDERSTAND.' 14 IN THEM IS FULFILLED THE PROPHECY OF ISAIAH: 'YOU WILL BE EVER HEARING BUT NEVER UNDERSTANDING; YOU WILL BE EVER SEEING BUT NEVER PERCEIVING. 15 FOR THIS PEOPLE'S HEART HAS BECOME CALLOUSED; THEY HARDLY HEAR WITH THEIR EARS, AND THEY HAVE CLOSED THEIR EYES. OTHERWISE THEY MIGHT SEE WITH THEIR EYES, HEAR WITH THEIR EARS, UNDERSTAND WITH THEIR HEARTS AND TURN, AND I WOULD HEAL THEM.' 16 BUT BLESSED ARE YOUR EYES BECAUSE THEY SEE, AND YOUR EARS BECAUSE THEY HEAR. 17 FOR TRULY I TELL YOU, MANY PROPHETS AND RIGHTEOUS PEOPLE LONGED TO SEE WHAT YOU SEE BUT DID NOT SEE IT, AND TO HEAR WHAT YOU HEAR BUT DID NOT HEAR IT."

How do we handle this kind of adversity? What does it teach us about our growth and development? What does God want us to understand about ourselves and the way we respond to resistance?

Jesus is going to help us.